COME AND JOIN US!

18 Holidays Celebrated All Year Long

written by **Liz Kleinrock**

illustrated by **Chaaya Prabhat**

HARPER

An Imprint of HarperCollinsPublishers

Special thanks to Parrish Turner, Jenny Ly, and all the
readers who provided invaluable feedback for this book.

Come and Join Us!: 18 Holidays Celebrated All Year Long
Copyright © 2023 by HarperCollins Publishers
Written by Elizabeth Kleinrock
Illustrations by Chaaya Prabhat
All rights reserved. Manufactured in Italy.
No part of this book may be used or reproduced in any manner whatsoever without
written permission except in the case of brief quotations embodied in critical articles
and reviews. For information address HarperCollins Children's Books, a division of
HarperCollins Publishers, 195 Broadway, New York, NY 10007.
www.harpercollinschildrens.com
Library of Congress Control Number: 2022940854
ISBN 978-0-06-314447-7

The artist used Photoshop to create the digital illustrations for this book.
Typography by Rachel Zegar
23 24 25 26 27   RTLO   10 9 8 7 6 5 4 3 2 1
First Edition

To the Phenomenal Young Starz, the
Dabbing Pigs, the Weirdos, and every
student I've had the privilege of teaching.

—Liz

Welcome to our classroom! You've arrived at just the right time to celebrate the holidays with us.

When picturing the holidays, a lot of people think about winter, presents, decorated trees, and everything colored red and green. Maybe you do too! But did you know that there are holidays where people gather to eat, pray, dance, sing, remember, and love one another happening all year round?

COME AND JOIN US!

I'm Jenny and I love to celebrate Seollal, the Korean

LUNAR NEW YEAR!

Even though we are far from our relatives across the ocean, my cousins and I wear our hanbok and honor our ancestors by offering food in a charye ceremony.

When we eat, I try to devour as many bowls of ddeokguk as I can hold.

I always look forward to playing yutnori and flying kites in the sky.

I also celebrate Lunar New Year with my friend Grace. Her family is Chinese American and we watch the lion dancers parade through the streets in her neighborhood together.

Do you celebrate with PARADES for your holidays?

The name's Cody and the
MARDI GRAS
parade is magical!

This holiday is also called *Fat Tuesday*, and it marks the last day before the beginning of Lent. During the forty days of Lent, some people don't eat meat and others give up something they enjoy, so we spend this holiday feasting on all the things we love to eat—and then some.

I sit on my dad's shoulders to see the parade and the crowded, music-filled streets.

At dinner, we watch festival-goers in their colorful costumes from our window, and we hold our own celebration with my favorite meal: gumbo and beignets!

Are your celebrations COLORFUL?

My name is Krish and
HOLI
is the most colorful of holidays.

We light bonfires for puja, shower each other with love, and chase away all things bad and evil.

A rainbow of colors fills the air while my friends and I splash each other with water balloons.

At night, my family gathers to eat and, just before I fall asleep, I can still taste thandai on my tongue.

Do you STAY UP LATE for any of your holidays?

My name is Nasim and I stay
up to ring in
NOWRUZ,
the Persian New Year!

Before the new year, we celebrate Charshanbe Suri, known as the festival of fire. We dance and sing traditional songs about flames taking away our ills and bringing us warmth. I even jump over small pits of fire.

Nowruz is all about renewal and fresh starts. We clean every corner of our home, top to bottom, and fill boxes to donate.

The best part? For thirteen days, the kids in my family visit our elders and finish welcoming the new year with a giant picnic.

Do you GATHER WITH FAMILY to celebrate your holidays?

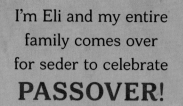

I'm Eli and my entire
family comes over
for seder to celebrate
PASSOVER!

My house is full of the smells of matzah ball
soup and the sound of joyful singing.

I love listening to the story of our Exodus from
Egypt that we tell together every year.

My cousins and I run from room to room, racing
to find the hidden afikomen to finish our meal.

When it's time, I open the door to invite the
prophet Elijah inside.

**How do your holidays
INVITE OTHERS to celebrate together?**

I'm Darsh and spending
VAISAKHI
with my entire community
is the best time of the year!

We come together to celebrate the joyful harvest and the birth of
the Khalsa.

In our Sikh tradition, my father helps me tie my patka, and my whole
family wears clothes of bright blue and saffron. We pray at our gurdwara
and then invite our friends and neighbors to join our parade! We cheer
as we wave at the floats decorated with bright fabrics and flowers.

**How do you
DECORATE for the holidays?**

I'm Lily and my family decorates our home with flowers and candles on
VESAK,
honoring Buddha's birthday, enlightenment, and death.

At night, my family hangs paper lanterns and also releases them into the sky, where they float up to join the stars.

I love to visit the temple to chant, meditate, and breathe in the smell of incense. On Vesak, we remember the importance of having compassion, and we perform acts of service for others.

How do you HELP AND SHOW CARE FOR OTHERS during your celebrations?

My name is Bryan and I love
JUNETEENTH
because it's all about caring
for our community and
celebrating freedom.

On June 19 in 1865, the last enslaved Black people in Texas learned that they were free—even though freedom had been promised to them two and half years before.

My uncle throws a *Freedom Day* barbecue for our family and friends. We eat red foods like yummy red velvet cake and red punch. I also get the first spoonful of my aunt Mae's black-eyed peas! At night, we hold sparklers to the sky to remember those we lost and to celebrate the lives we have.

Together we sing and dance as we honor our ancestors.

Do you SING AND DANCE during your holidays?

I am Autumn and my
people love to sing and dance during
LUMBEE HOMECOMING.

Homecoming is very special to us because it used to be illegal for
my people to celebrate our heritage. We learned to hide our traditions
in plain sight by holding Homecoming near the Fourth of July. Many
other tribal nations celebrate together during this time too.

During Homecoming, I race to hug my friends and family who are
visiting from out of town. All over the neighborhood, people greet each
other, and the smell of fry bread and collard sandwiches fills the air.

We gather to watch performance art as dancers move in rhythm
with the drums.

**How do you celebrate
your holidays with ART?**

Priya here!
I love making art on
ONAM.

My brother and I help to create Onam pookalam—artwork made with bright flower petals. Together we collect flowers from our garden and carefully separate the petals as we lay them into beautiful designs.

We gather for a potluck dinner and the room bursts with people I love.

My dad tells his stories of the Vallamkali boat races in his youth while I skip in circles pretending to be the beloved King Mahabali!

Which holidays make you feel CONNECTED to your family?

My name is Ron and during
OBON
I feel connected to my family
members who lived before me.

During this festival, the spirits of our ancestors return to visit us.

At sundown, we light senko to call our ancestors back home, and we dance to the shakuhachi flute and taiko drums.

With my sister by my side in our yukata kimonos, we share shaved ice and watch the bon odori dancers move to the beat of the drums.

On the last day of the festival, we hold a Toro Nagashi ceremony. My family writes the names of our ancestors on paper lanterns and then watches the rolling waves carry them out into the ocean, guiding our ancestors back to their spiritual resting place.

How do your holidays bridge the
PAST AND PRESENT?

I'm Noa! When my family celebrates
ROSH HASHANAH
and **YOM KIPPUR,**
we reflect on our past actions and
words and look to the future.

On Rosh Hashanah, the shofar is blown to welcome the holiday. My brother and I count how long the final note lasts, but we sometimes run out of fingers.

My favorite treat is dipping apple slices into honey in hopes of a sweet new year.

Yom Kippur is our holiest day. We walk to the synagogue dressed in white. Some of the grown-ups in my family fast and we all apologize to anyone we might have hurt in the past year.

When nighttime comes, we break the fast with noodle kugel and bagels!

How do you celebrate the
NEW YEAR?

I'm Koa!
Here in Hawai'i, my community
celebrates our new year festival,

MAKAHIKI,

for four whole months!

During this holiday, my ancestors honored the god Lono and
took breaks from work to strengthen and care for their bodies.
These days, we come together for a luau, where we eat many
of the same foods as the ancient Hawaiians, like kālua pig.
At night, fireworks explode above the islands and create a
spectacle of lights to welcome in the new year.

What special TRADITIONS do you
keep for your holidays?

My name is Tristan
and my family has many traditions for
DÍA DE LOS MUERTOS!

My parents and I visit the graves of family members we have lost so we can reunite with their spirits.

I decorate our family's ofrenda with marigolds and photos of my abuelo. I also add my favorite food: tortas ahogadas!

The rest of our family joins us to share pan de muerto and watch the procession of calavera painted faces and listen to the mariachi bands. I try to stay up late but fall asleep listening to my abuela telling stories about our ancestors.

What kinds of STORIES do you tell on your holiday?

My name is Anika and
DIWALI
is packed with stories!

After cleaning up our home, I light the diyas with my family and together we snack on treats like halwa and ladoo. On Diwali, my auntie tells the story of the powerful Ravana with ten heads and twenty arms and his defeat by the brave lord Rama!

Diwali lasts for five days and reminds us of the triumph of good over evil. Snuggled close, we watch the shadows dance across the wall.

Which of your holidays use LIGHT to celebrate?

I'm Joy and on
KWANZAA
I watch the black, green, and red
candles of the kinara shine in
our window for seven days.

Each candle represents one of the Seven Principles called Nguzo Saba. We believe that each one will help us build community and lead us in our journey toward freedom.

I help set up the mkeka place mat with ears of corn, fruit, and the unity cup. Every evening, we read a book about Black history and talk about the values of Nguzo Saba. On the last day, we exchange zawadi, gifts that help us keep these values close.

What VALUES are uplifted on your holidays?

My name is Zanib and
RAMADAN
reminds me of the values of
righteousness, generosity,
kindness, and caring for our
community.

Islamic holidays follow the cycle of the moon, so the dates change every year. Muslim grown-ups do not eat or drink during daylight hours for a full month while we observe Ramadan. Not even water. This can be hard, but fasting and reflecting brings my family closer.

At the end of Ramadan, there's a celebration called Eid al-Fitr that lasts for three days. The whole family gathers in our new clothes to eat festive foods and go to Eid prayer services outside. I look forward to receiving gifts of money—called eidi—from my elders.

Which of your holidays include GIFT GIVING and receiving?

On every holiday we celebrate, the best gift is spending time with the people we love.

And even though we have our school vacation in the winter, December holidays aren't the most important for everyone.

In fact, every day is a celebration in
our beautiful community.

COME AND JOIN US!

AUTHOR'S NOTE

Dear reader,

Growing up as a Jewish kid, I celebrated our High Holy Day season in early autumn. I loved spending this time with my family. When December rolled around and I shared with friends and classmates that I didn't celebrate Christmas, I was met with comments such as "That's so weird" and "I feel so sorry for you." They were unable to understand that my family didn't decorate a tree or write to Santa. These reactions often made me feel uncomfortable, like my peers were looking down on my family and our beliefs and practices for not matching their own.

I wrote this book to encourage people who celebrate what I call "dominant culture holidays" to be inclusive and respectful of holidays beyond their own. If you go to a grocery store, will you see decorations and displays for your holiday? Will the music you hear celebrate your holiday? Will people's greetings to you acknowledge your holiday? How do you think it might make people feel if they've never had these experiences? Answering these questions is the first step toward decentering one's own holidays and embracing others as equally important.

Eighteen holidays from a myriad of religions and cultures were highlighted here, but there are so many more that are celebrated throughout the year by our neighbors and peers. And although the pages of this book aren't able to hold every holiday, I wish for someone to feel a little more seen after reading it. I want children whose holiday celebrations fall outside of December to know that their festivities are beautiful and meaningful. Do not dim your own light because of others' ignorance. Represent your cultures and beliefs with pride.

Love,
Liz

From creating inclusive lessons to amplifying texts about different faiths and beliefs to advocating for an inclusive school calendar, we can all support students and children of nondominant faiths and identities. Parents, caregivers, and educators can visit www.teachandtransform.org/resources for more information on decentering winter holidays.

GLOSSARY

SEOLLAL
lunar: Determined by the moon
hanbok: Traditional Korean clothing
charye: A ritual in which food is prepared and offered to ancestors
ddeokguk: A New Year's soup made with sliced rice cakes
yutnori: A traditional game played with sticks

MARDI GRAS

Lent: A forty day period when Christians fast, pray, and give back to their communities

HOLI

puja: Hindu worship rituals

thandai: A refreshing drink made with milk and flavorful spices

NOWRUZ

Charshanbe Suri: A festival that takes place on the last Wednesday of the Persian solar year

PASSOVER

seder: A Jewish ritual meal on the first nights of Passover. Seder means *order*.

matzah ball soup: Soup with dumplings made from matzah meal

Exodus: A mass departure of people. In the Torah, the Exodus tells the story of the liberation of the Jewish people from Egypt.

afikomen: A piece of matzah that is often hidden for children to find and is later eaten at the end of the meal

Elijah: A highly revered prophet in Judaism

VAISAKHI

Khalsa: A community of Sikh people

Sikh: A person who believes in the religion of Sikhism

patka: Headwear worn by Sikhs

gurdwara: A place of worship for Sikhs

VESAK

Buddha: The founder of Buddhism

incense: Fragrance that is burned, typically in the form of a stick or cone

JUNETEENTH

enslave: To force a person or group of people to work without pay and/or to restrict freedom

LUMBEE HOMECOMING

Lumbee Tribe: An Indigenous* tribe residing in the land known as North Carolina

Indigenous: Native to the land, also known as First Nations, Native American, and American Indian within the United States

ONAM

Onam pookalam: Patterns and designs made with flowers and flower petals

Vallamkali: A traditional Indian boat race

King Mahabali: A kind king from Hindu history

OBON

senko: Japanese incense sticks

shakuhachi flute and taiko drums: Traditional Japanese musical instruments

kimonos: The traditional dress of Japan

bon odori: A Japanese folk dance to welcome and honor the spirits of the dead

Toro Nagashi: A traditional custom in which candlelit paper lanterns are released into a body of water to symbolize the guiding of the souls of the deceased toward peace

ROSH HASHANAH & YOM KIPPUR

shofar: An instrument traditionally made from the horn of a ram blown on the Jewish New Year

synagogue: A Jewish place of worship

kugel: Baked pudding or casserole typically made of noodles or potato, from the Ashkenazi tradition

MAKAHIKI

Lono: The Hawaiian god of agriculture, fertility, rainfall, music, and peace

luau: A Hawaiian party or feast

kālua: A traditional Hawaiian cooking method using an imu (underground oven)

DÍA DE LOS MUERTOS

ofrenda: An altar to honor lost loved ones

abuelo / abuela: Grandfather / Grandmother

tortas ahogadas: A Mexican sandwich made with salsa, meat, and onions

pan de muerto: Mexican sweet bread made for Día de los Muertos

calavera: A representation of a human skull, also known as La Catrina

mariachi: A traditional Mexican folk music

DIWALI

diyas: Oil lamps

hawla: A dessert made with grated vegetables cooked with ghee, sugar, and milk

ladoo: A ball-shaped sweet made with flour, fat, and sugar

Ravana: A multiheaded demon king in Hindu mythology

Rama: A major deity in Hinduism believed to be the seventh incarnation of the God Vishnu

KWANZAA

kinara: A seven-branched candleholder used in Kwanzaa celebrations

Nguzo Saba: The Seven Principles in African and African American culture: Umoja (Unity), Kujichagulia (Self-Determination), Ujima (Collective Work and Responsibility), Ujamaa (Cooperative Economics), Nia (Purpose), Kuumba (Creativity), and Imani (Faith)

mkeka: A decorative ceremonial mat

zawadi: Handmade gifts given on the last day of Kwanzaa

RAMADAN & EID AL-FITR

Islamic: Relating to the religion of Islam

Muslim: A person who believes in the religion of Islam

fasting: Limiting or abstaining from food or drink

eidi: Gifts given to children by older members of the family as part of Eid al-Fitr and Eid al-Adha